The Heart

Story by Steven Warrington MD, PhD
Illustration by Abigail Tan

Hi, I'm a heart. Not just any heart, but THE HEART! You only get one of me. It makes me pretty special.

There is even a day of the year called Valentine's day where a lot of people like to make each other cards with my picture drawn on it! It's a way of showing someone you care about them.

This is how everyone loooooooves to draw me, but I don't really look like this.

They even draw me without anything on!

Don't look, I'm naked!

They get the pinky red color right,
but the shape is all wrong

Even though I live inside you and don't wear stuff like shorts or shoes I still have a coat that goes around me. It is soooo fancy it even has a special name. It's called my pericardium. It's like a big balloon that I sit all snug in.

It's just for me and I stay inside it right in your chest.
Luckily, I'm not alone in you, my friends the lungs
stay right by my side.

The three of us are best friends and
work together all the time.
They don't have a fancy coat like me though.

But like they say, it's not what's on the outside that matters.
Did you know I have insides just like you do?

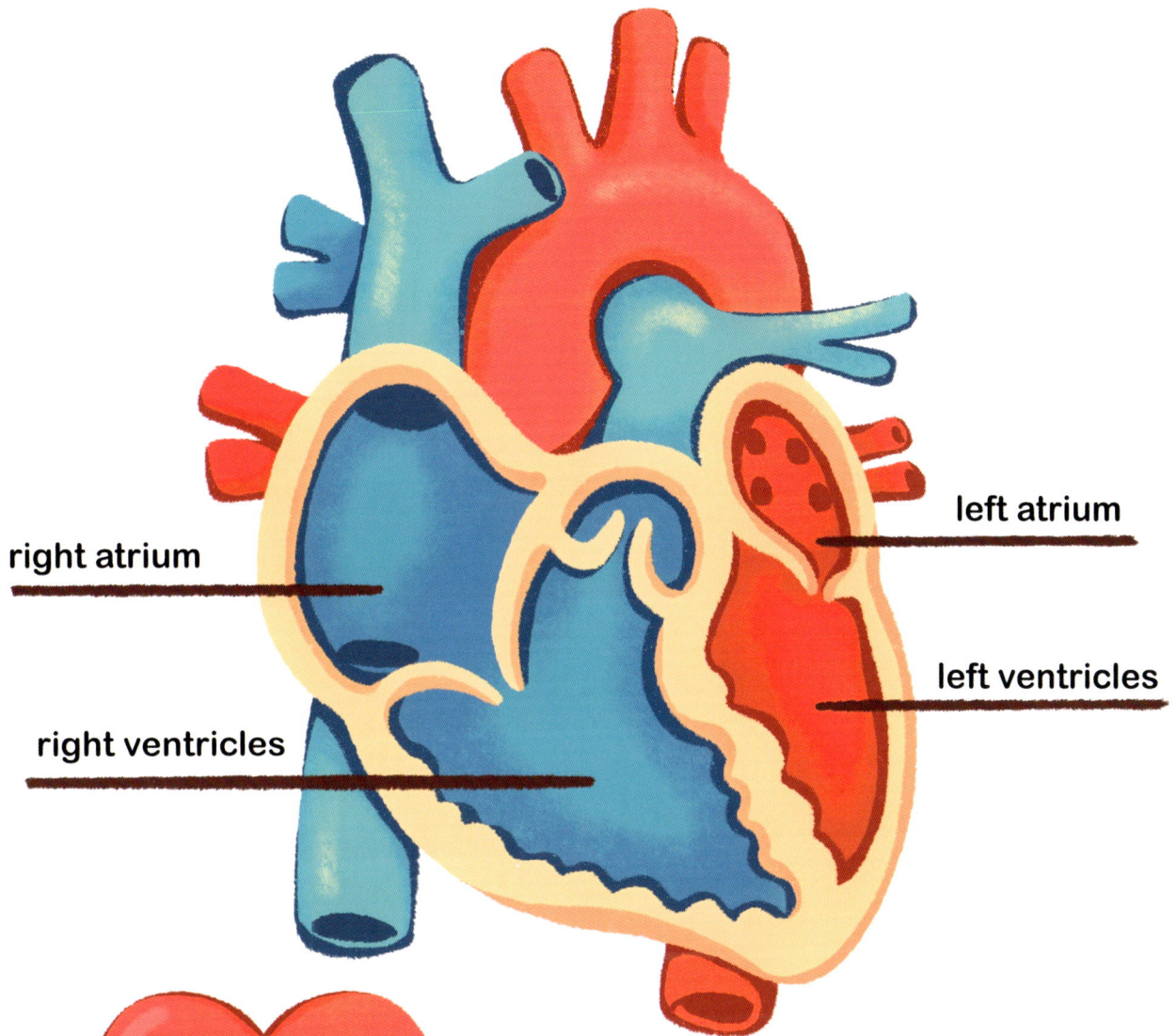

right atrium

left atrium

left ventricles

right ventricles

I have four big rooms inside me,
two on top and two on bottom.
The top two are called atrium and
the bottom two are called ventricles.

I even have doors between my rooms called valves.
It's all one way though, no going backwards!

I have to keep
things moving,
so I squeeze.
When I squeeze
it pushes the blood
and cells in me along,
that's called
the heartbeat.

After each squeeze
I take a break and relax

Should have called it
the heart squeeze
if you ask me.

I even squeeze in my sleep!

Squeezing pushes everything forward and
makes it go through tubes to the rest of the body.
Those tubes are called your blood vessels.
You might have even seen them before.

Have you ever noticed them on the top of your hand
or the different color inside your arms? That's them!

Since you've seen the blood vessels
do you want to feel me squeeze?
You can tell I'm squeezing by feeling
your wrist or your neck.

That thump thump you feel is your heart
pushing blood through the blood vessels.
The number of times you feel the beat
in a minute is called your pulse.

Doctors like to feel the thump thump to check up on me.

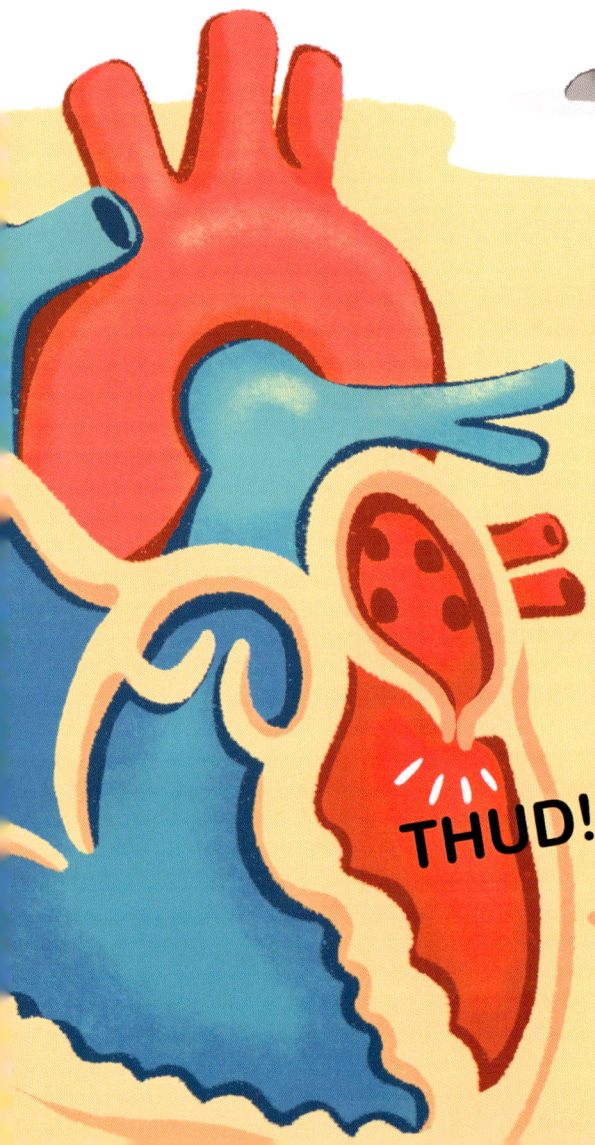

THUD!

THUD!

They also listen to the noises my doors make when they slam shut as I squeeze and relax.

I can get sick
just like you.
If I do I have to
go to the doctor.

Sometimes
it's because
I'm out of shape.

I'm too tired
to work hard.

Other times
I just get stiff.

That's
as far as
I can go.

That's why you have to keep me healthy, so I can keep squeezing great. You can keep me healthy by exercising.

Eating healthy food is important also.

Okay, for my heart.

When you exercise, I do too.
I squeeze faster and it helps keep me healthy.
Feel for me the next time you run and play.

If you treat me good and keep me healthy,
I'll grow with you and keep you healthy.
Now that you know who I am we can be best friends!

Atrium -
The top rooms
(chambers)
of the heart.

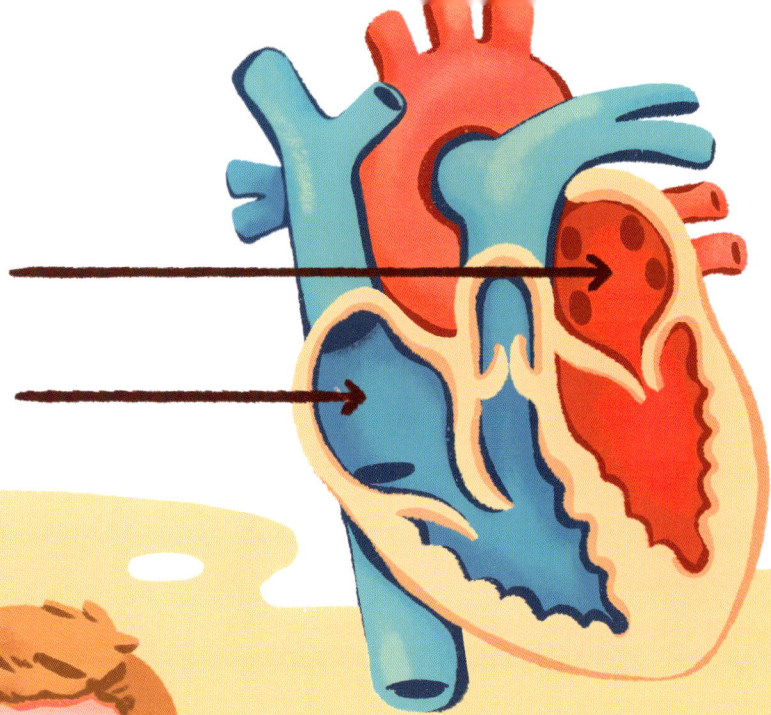

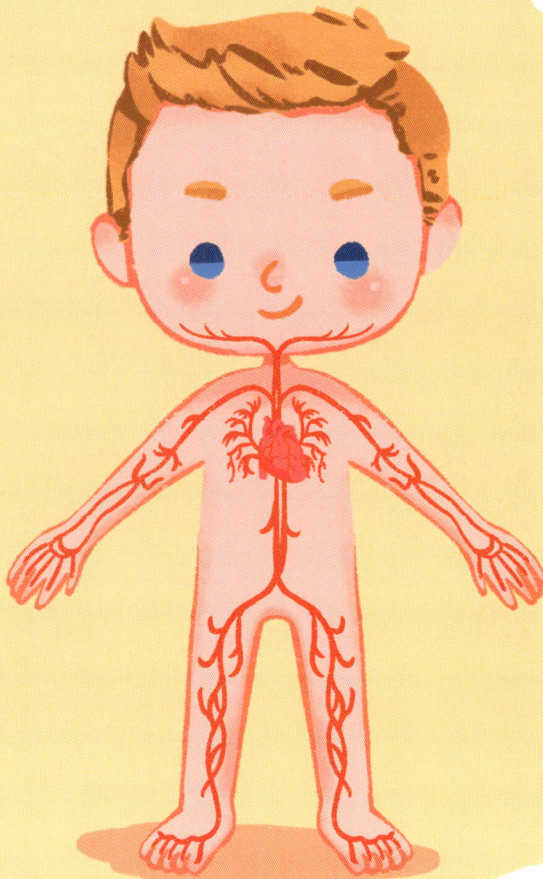

Blood Vessels –
The tubes that
let the heart push
blood around
the body.

Pericardium –
A coat (membrane)
that the heart sits in.

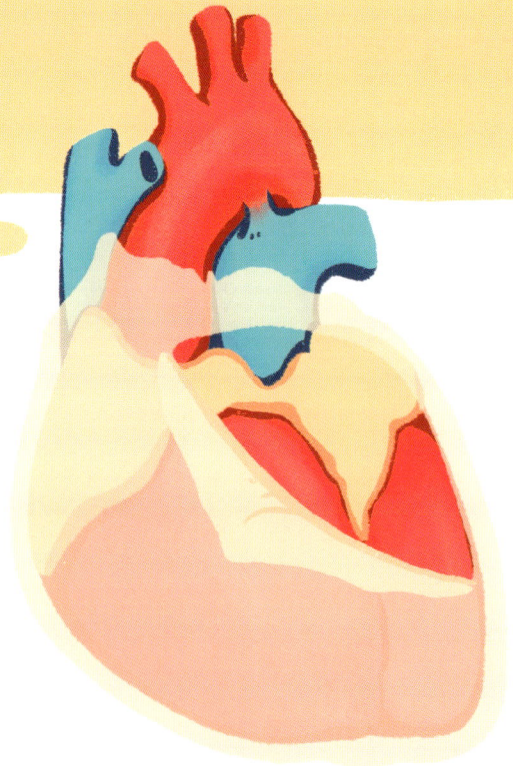

Pulse –
How many heartbeats
happen in a minute.

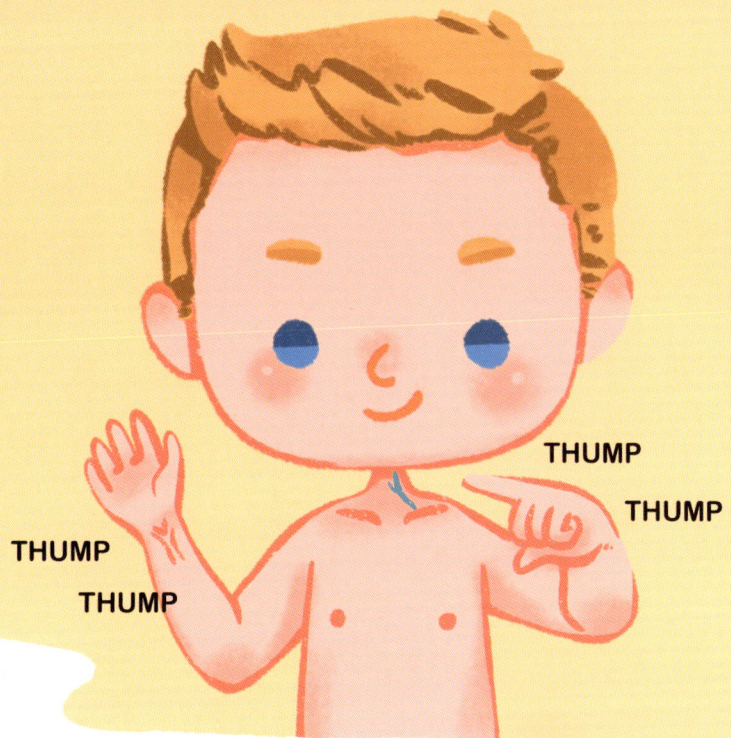

THUMP
THUMP

THUMP
THUMP

Valves –
The doors
between the rooms.
In a healthy heart
they only let
blood and cells
go in one direction.

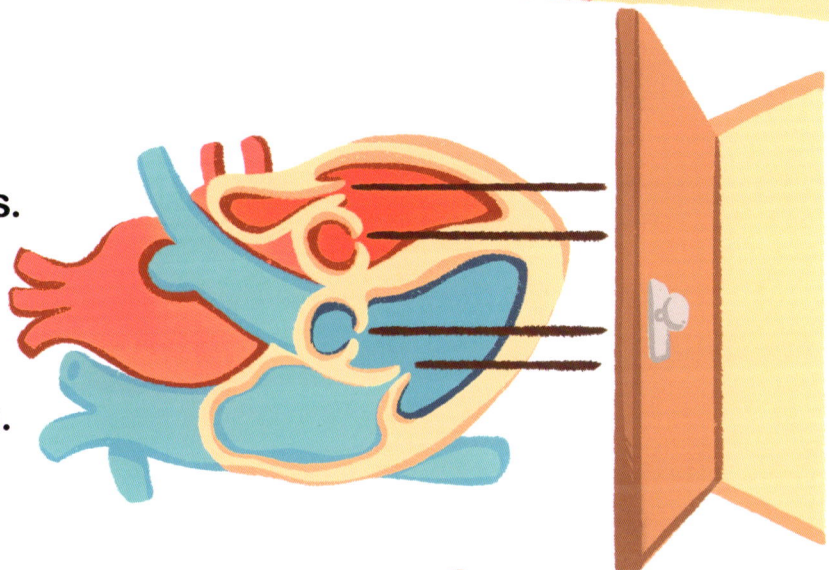

Ventricles –
The bottom rooms
(chambers) of the heart.

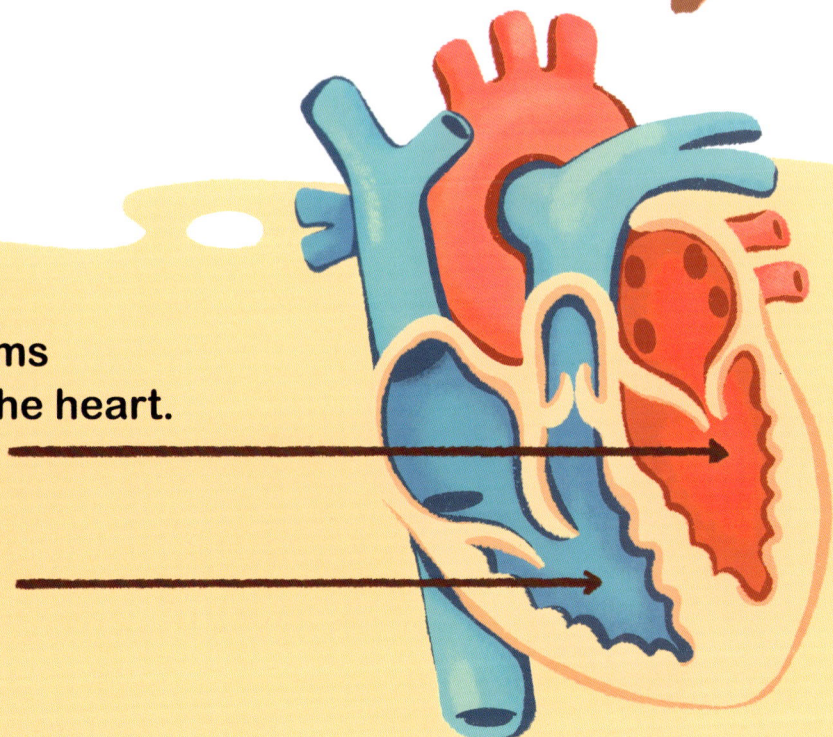

The Lungs

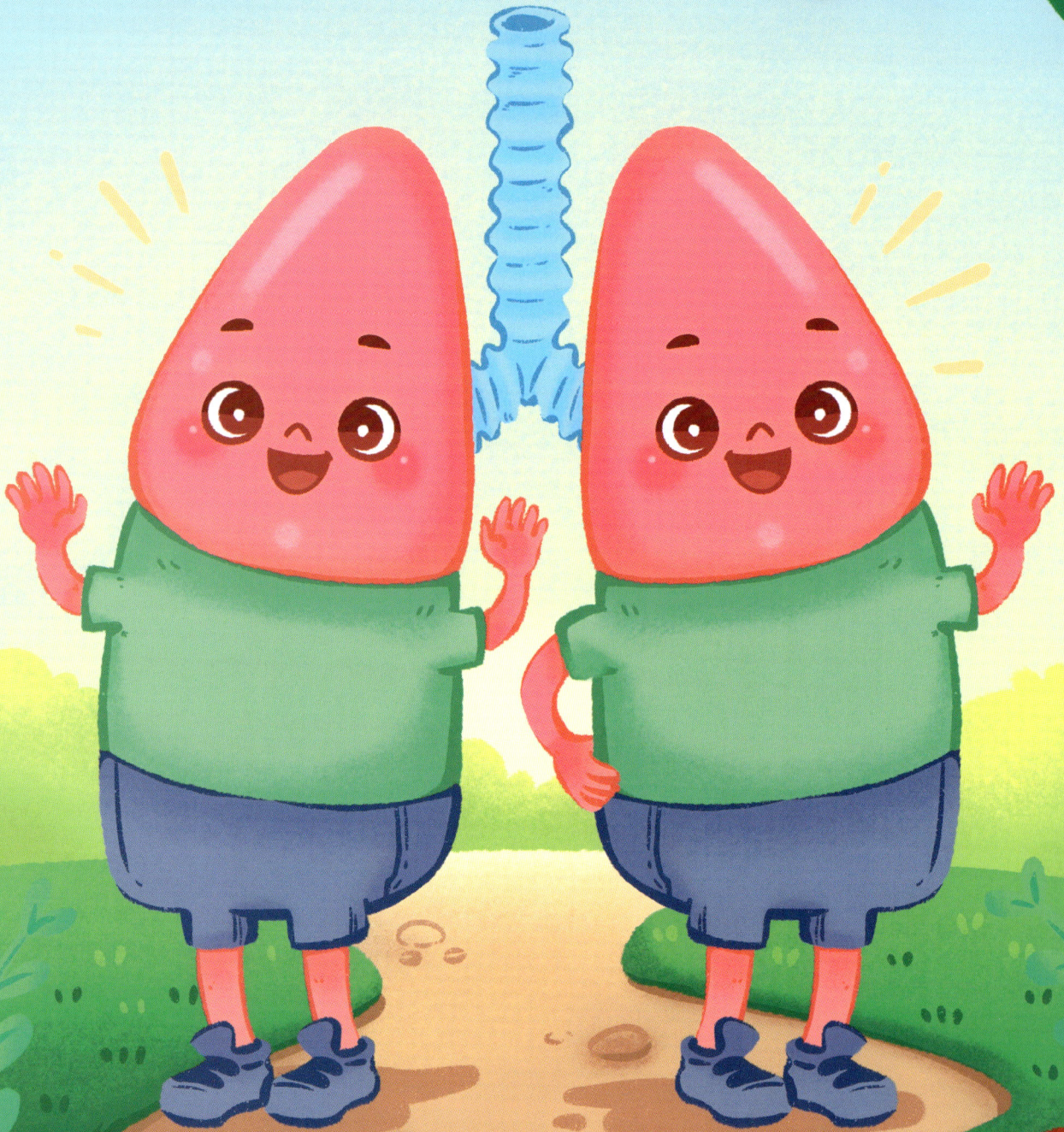

Story by Steven Warrington MD
Illustration by Abigail Tan

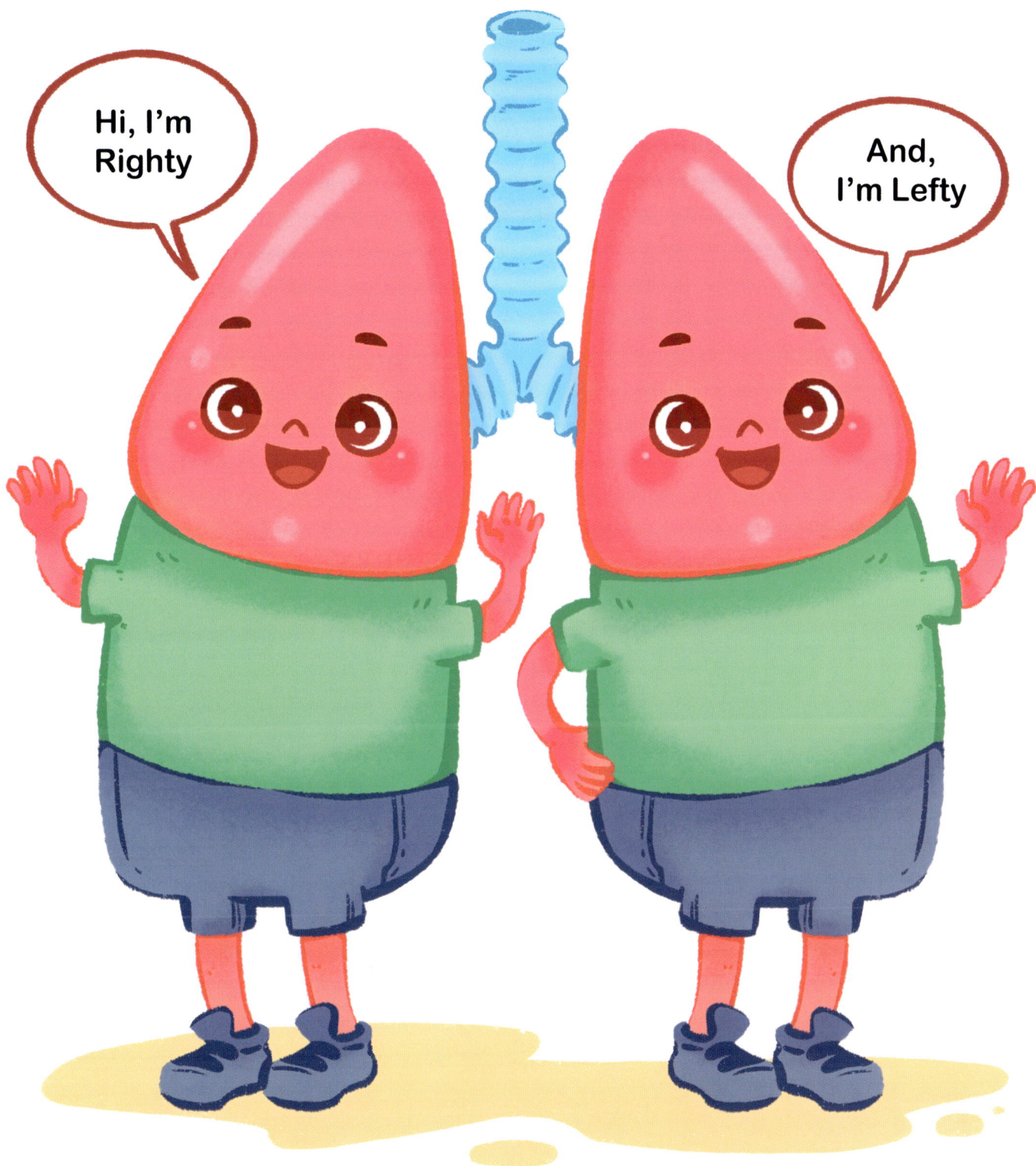

We sit next to each other inside of you.
The heart is our friend and sits in here with us too.
All of us are nice and cozy in your chest.

HOME SWEET CHEST

Even though
we look the same,
we aren't.

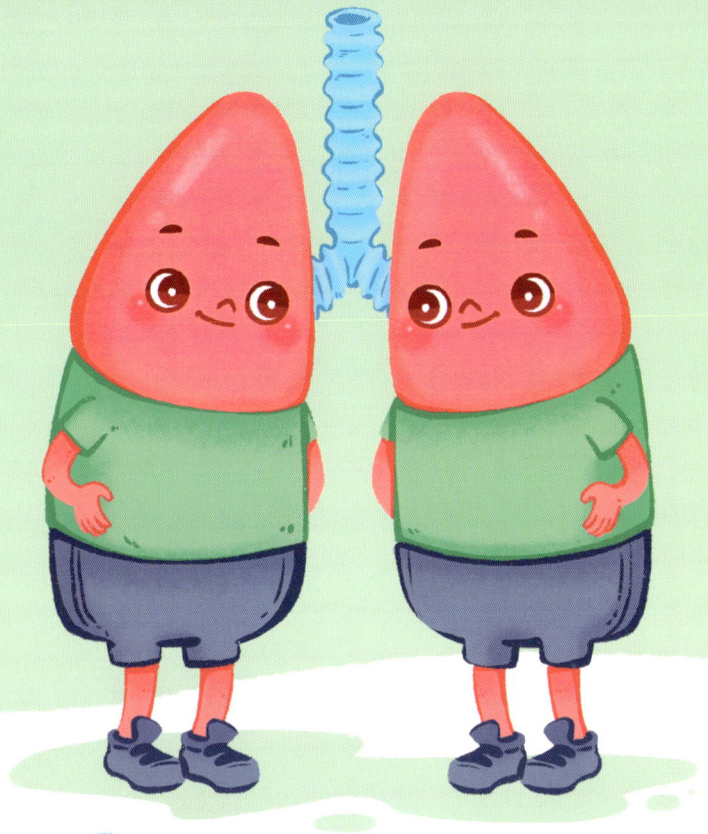

The right lung
has 3 parts to it.

The left lung
only has 2 parts.

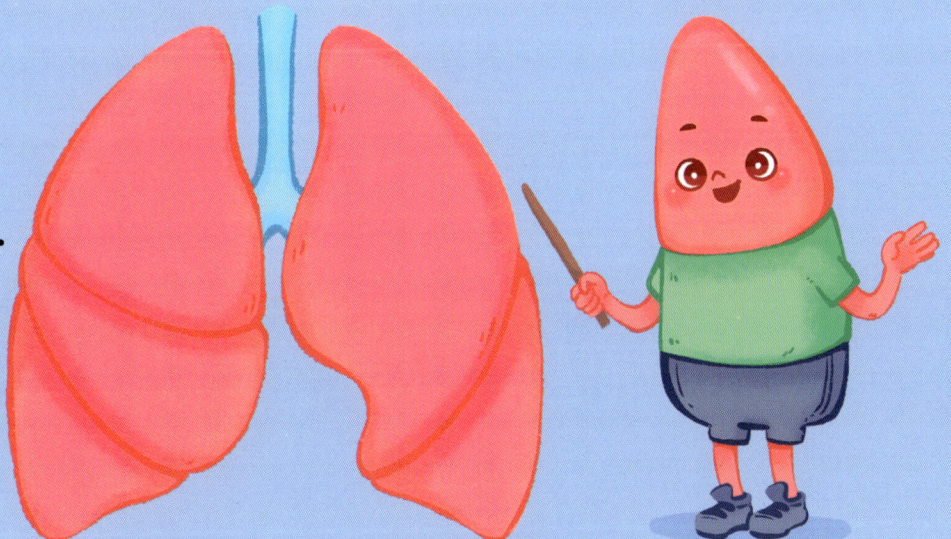

We work together to help you breathe.
Air comes in your nose or mouth,
and then it runs through a tube called the trachea.

The trachea links us together and is how
you get that air all the way down to us lungs.

When you take
a breath in
we get BIGGER,
because we are
full of air.

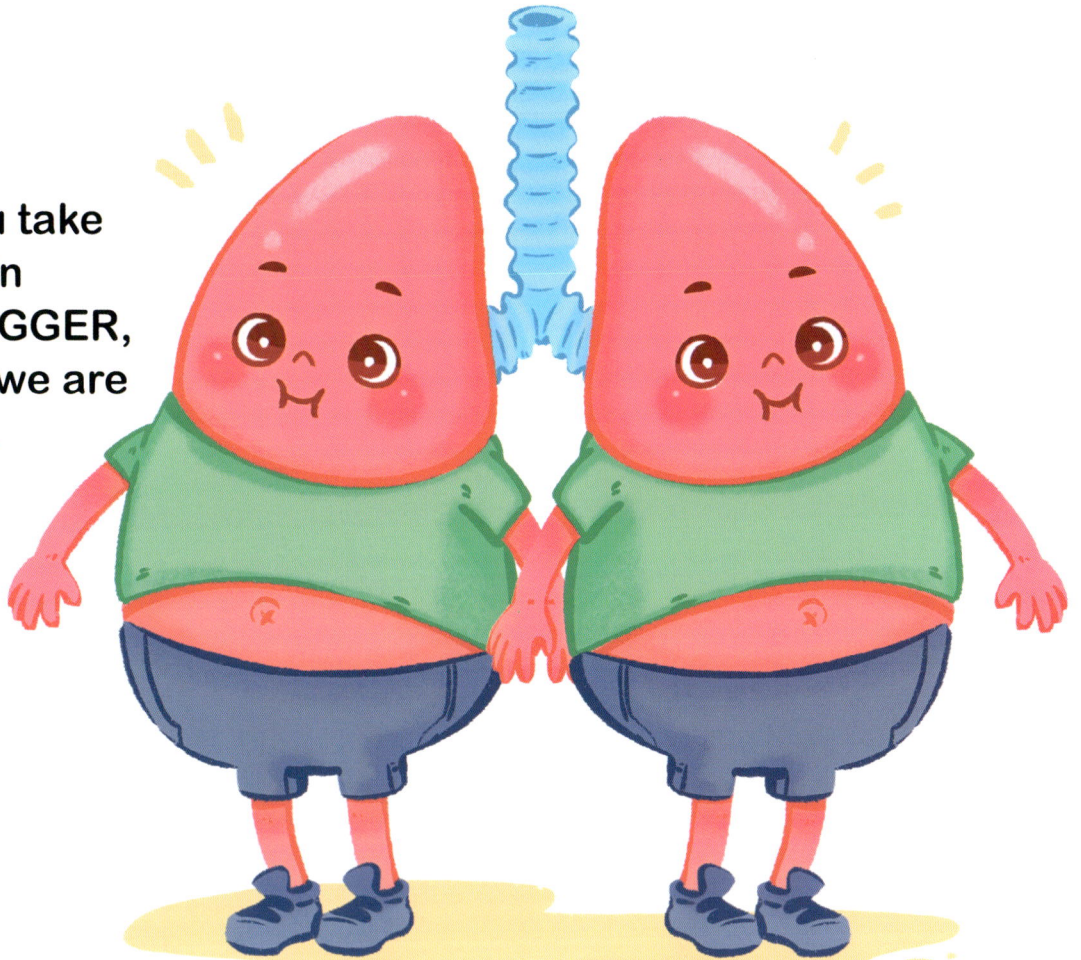

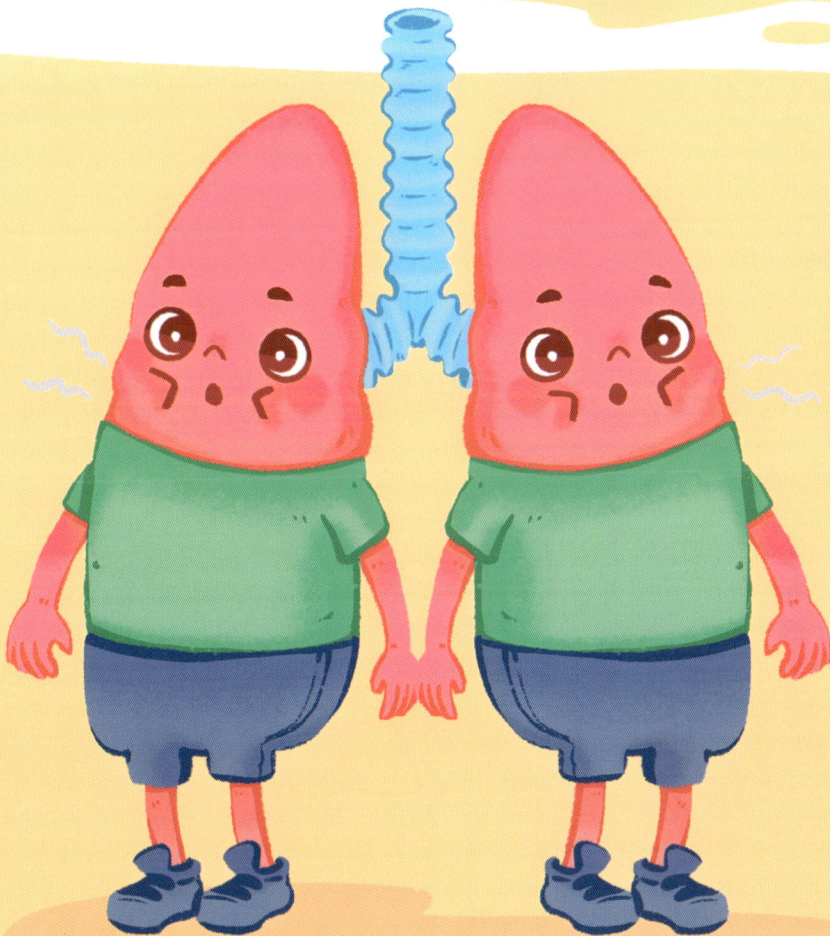

Then we get
smaller when you
breathe out air.

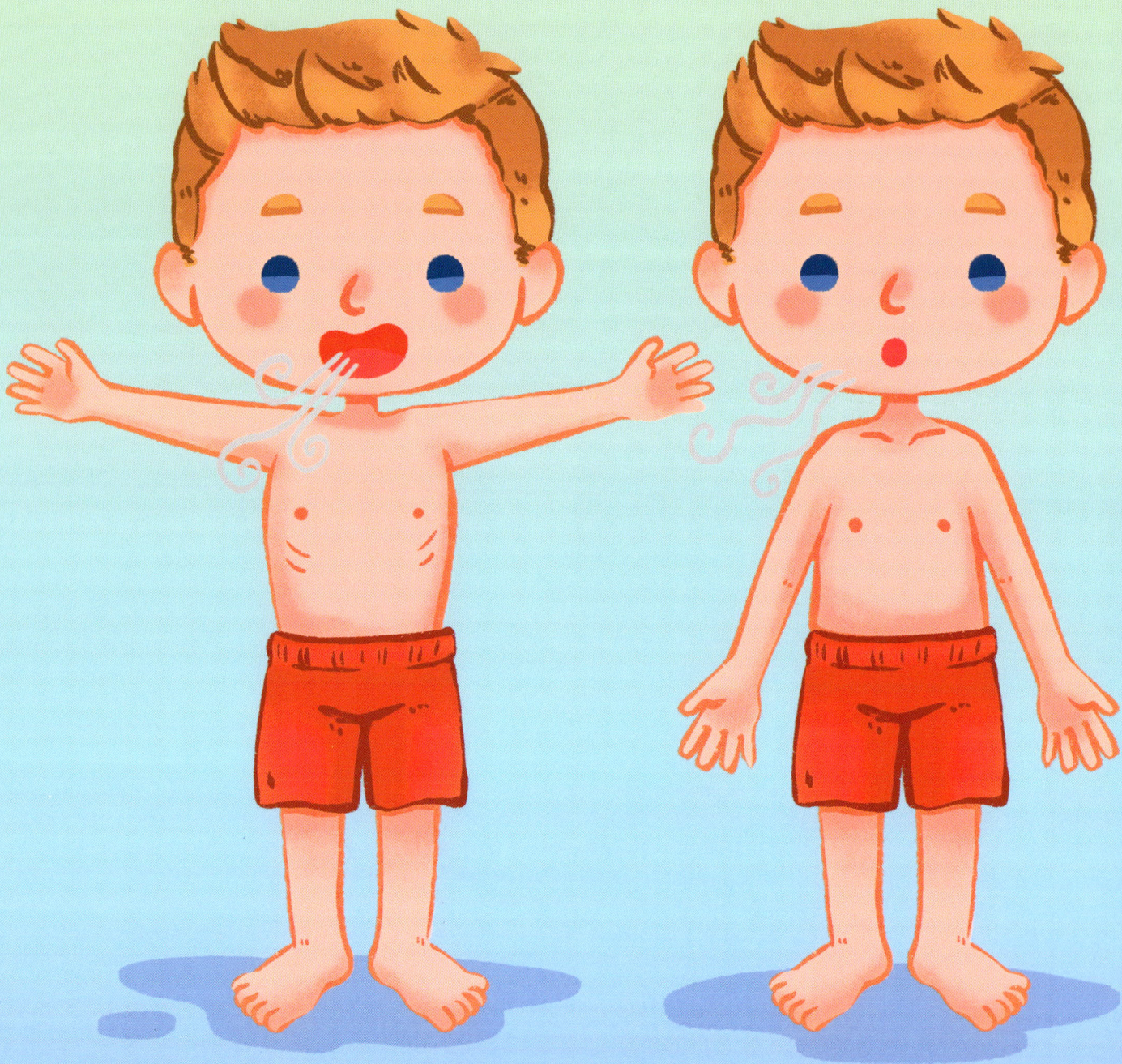

Even though you don't see us move,
if you watch your body you can see your chest get
bigger and smaller when you breathe in and out.
Sometimes you might even see the space between your ribs,
or above your collarbone, suck in as you breathe in.

It might not seem like it, but breathing is a lot of work and takes a ton of energy. A grown up usually takes between 12 and 20 breaths per minute, but a baby can breathe in and out up to 60 times a minute!

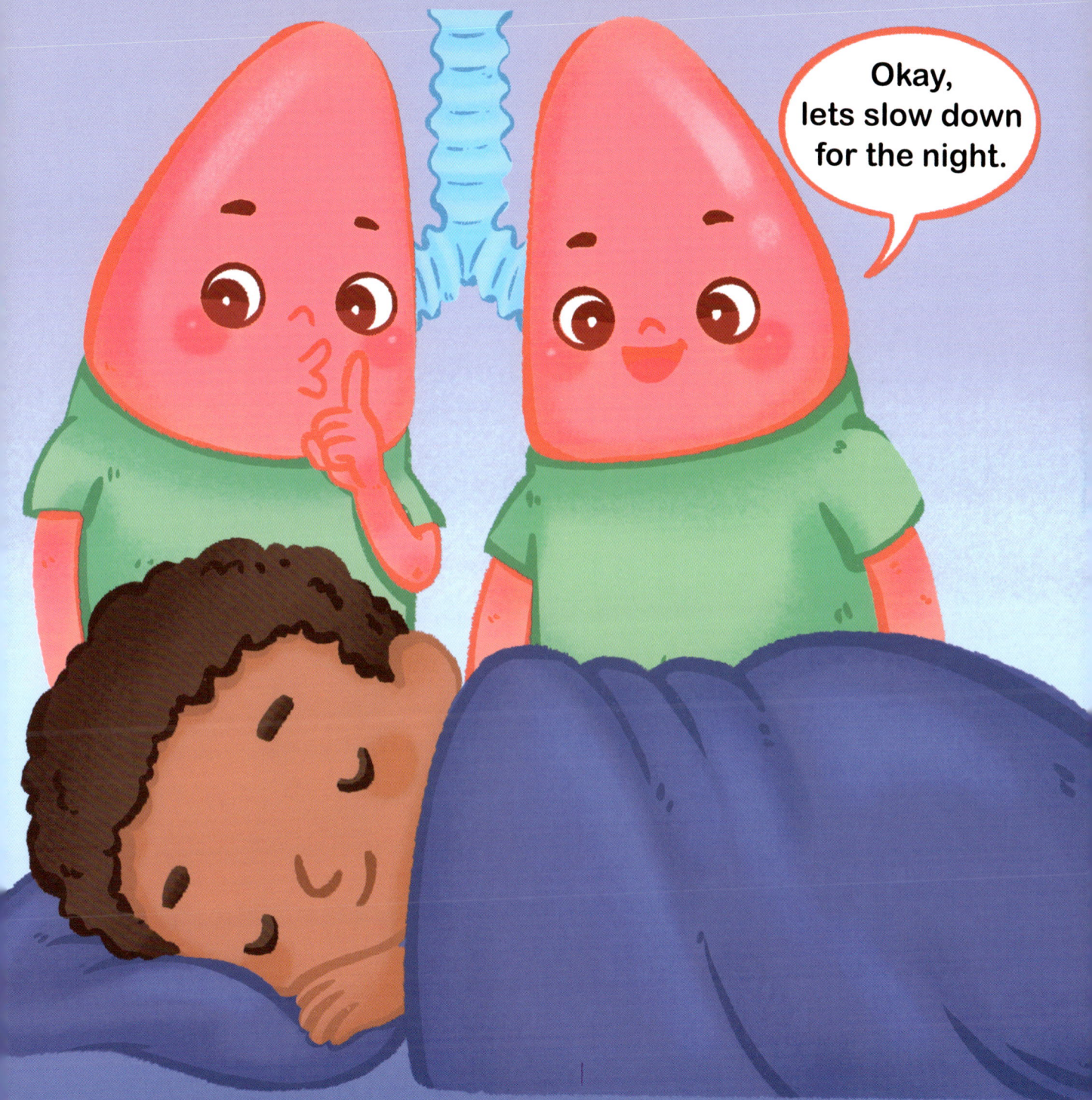

Okay, lets slow down for the night.

That means you will probably breathe in and out more than 20,000 times today! I'll let you in on a secret though, when you go to sleep we breathe a little bit slower.

We aren't just used for breathing though, we help you talk, laugh, and sing!

How was your day?

Can you think of any other fun stuff we help you do?

Have you ever tried holding your breath?

What about playing a harmonica or blowing bubbles?

To do those things we have
to get air in and out.
So the air goes down
the trachea and then
in and out through
the tube on our side
called the bronchus.

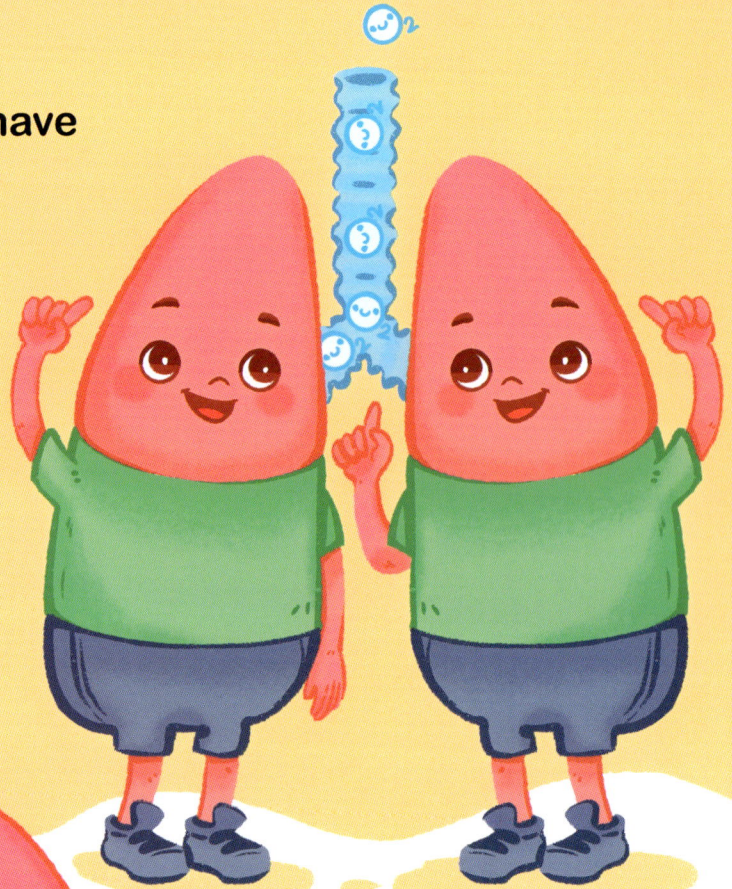

It's like
a maze in me.

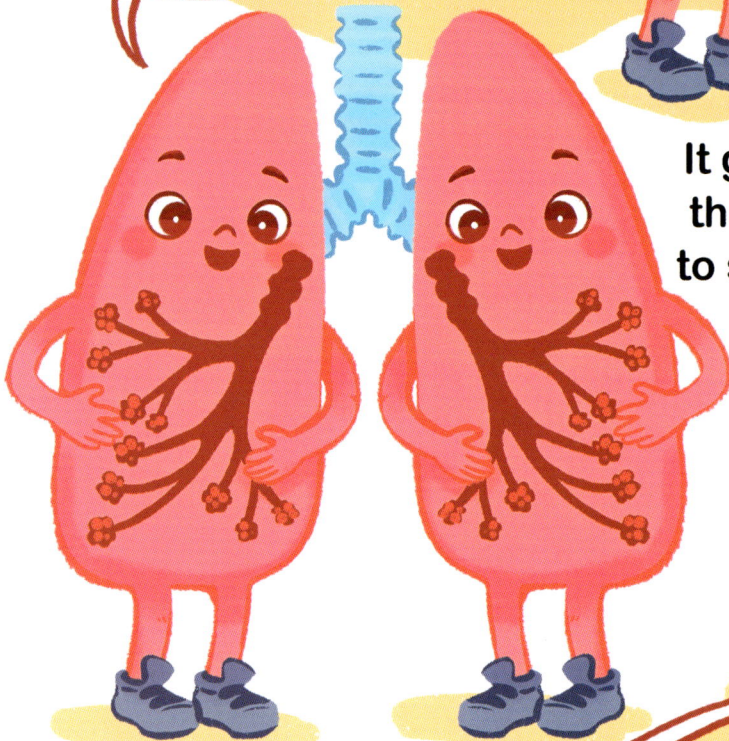

It goes through lots of tubes
that get smaller and smaller
to spread out and make sure
everywhere gets air.

Nice to meet you,
we are the alveoli.

Those tubes have lots of
little rooms at the end that
are like air bubbles.
They are called alveoli.

Even though they look like the fun packing bubbles that you get to pop, these alveoli have a big job.

They let the oxygen from the air
you breathe get to the rest of your body
because of their thin special walls.

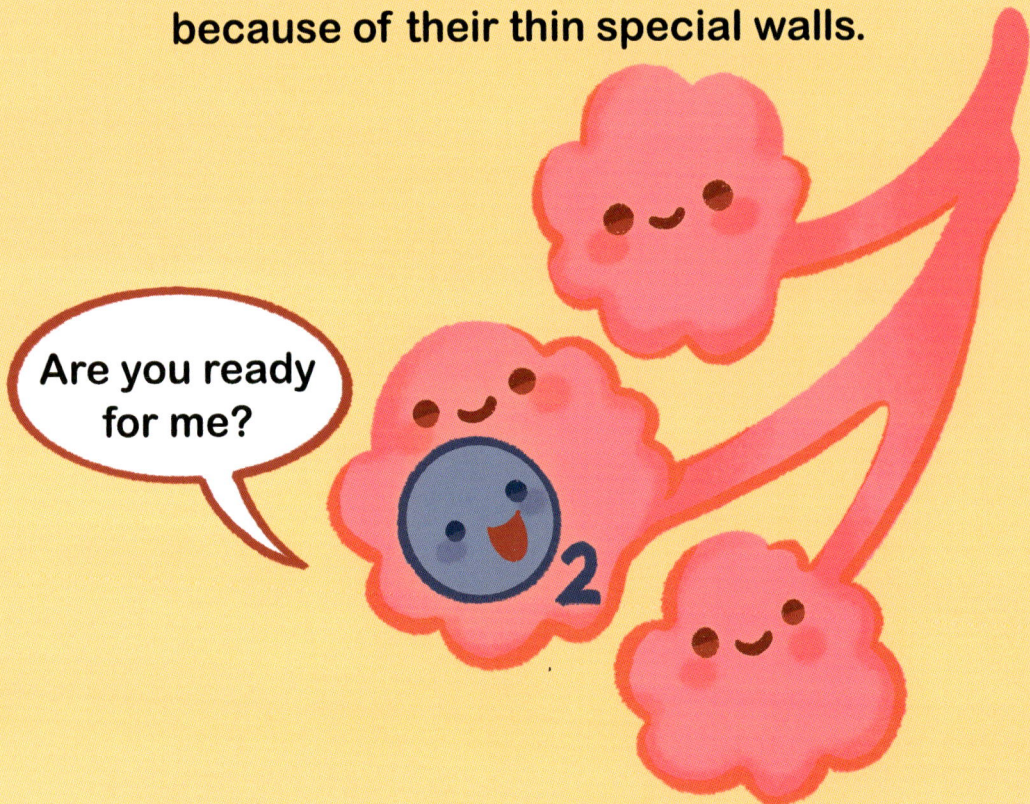

Are you ready
for me?

O₂

After you use the oxygen they also help
get rid of the stuff you can't use called carbon dioxide
so you can breathe it back out.

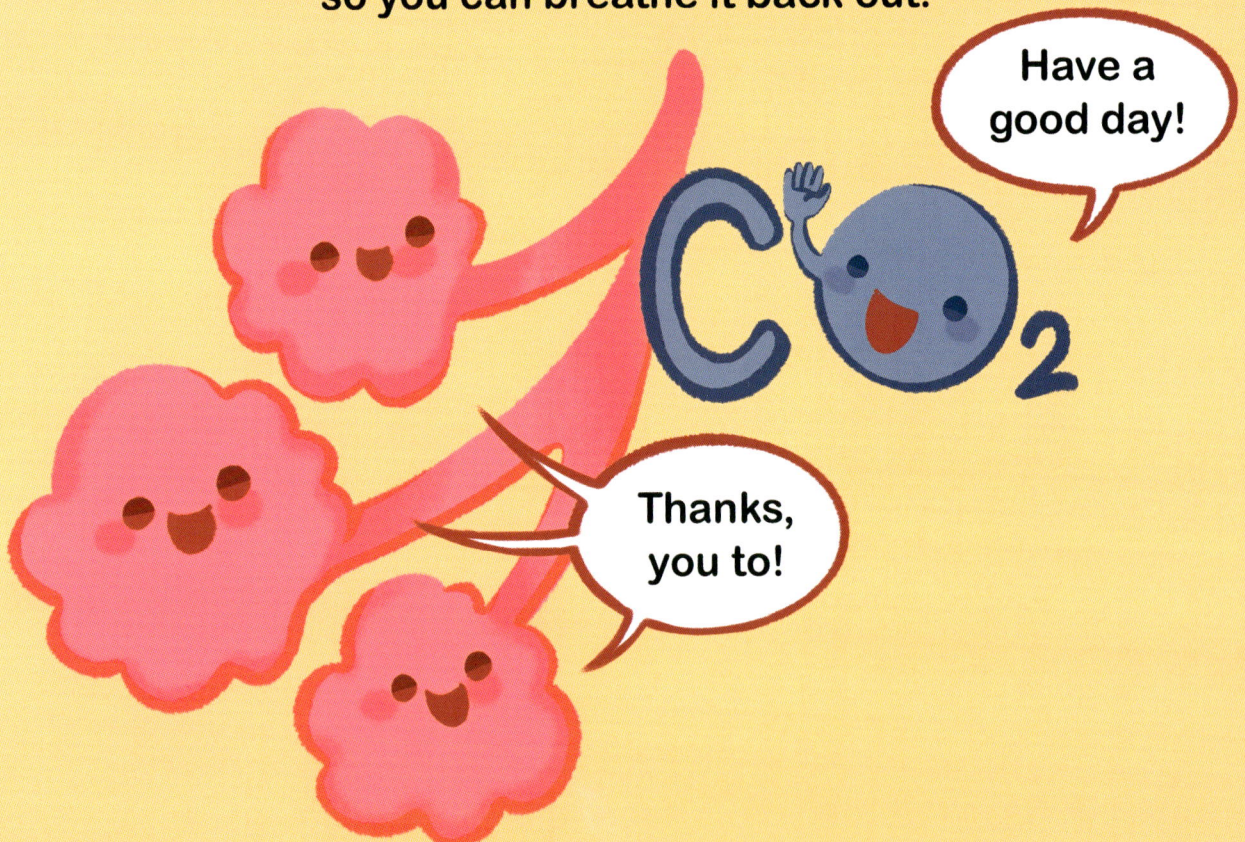

Have a
good day!

CO₂

Thanks,
you to!

Lungs and alveoli do their jobs best with clean air.
It keeps us and them healthy.

Ah, this air is sooooo fresh and good!

When the air is dirty or if you smoke
it makes it harder for us to work.
It even breaks down our walls stopping you
from using oxygen or getting that used carbon dioxide out.

This is broken,
I can't get through.

CO_2

Your body tries to keep those alveoli walls
from being broken. One of the ways it tries to stop
dirt and smoke from getting there is by having
the walls and floors lined with stuff called mucus.

Help,
I'm stuck.

Mucus is like sticky boogers. It keeps germs
and dirt from getting deeper in the lungs.

Instead of having hair outside like you do,
we have hair inside of us. Its another way
your body tries to keep yucky stuff out.
Our hair even moves!

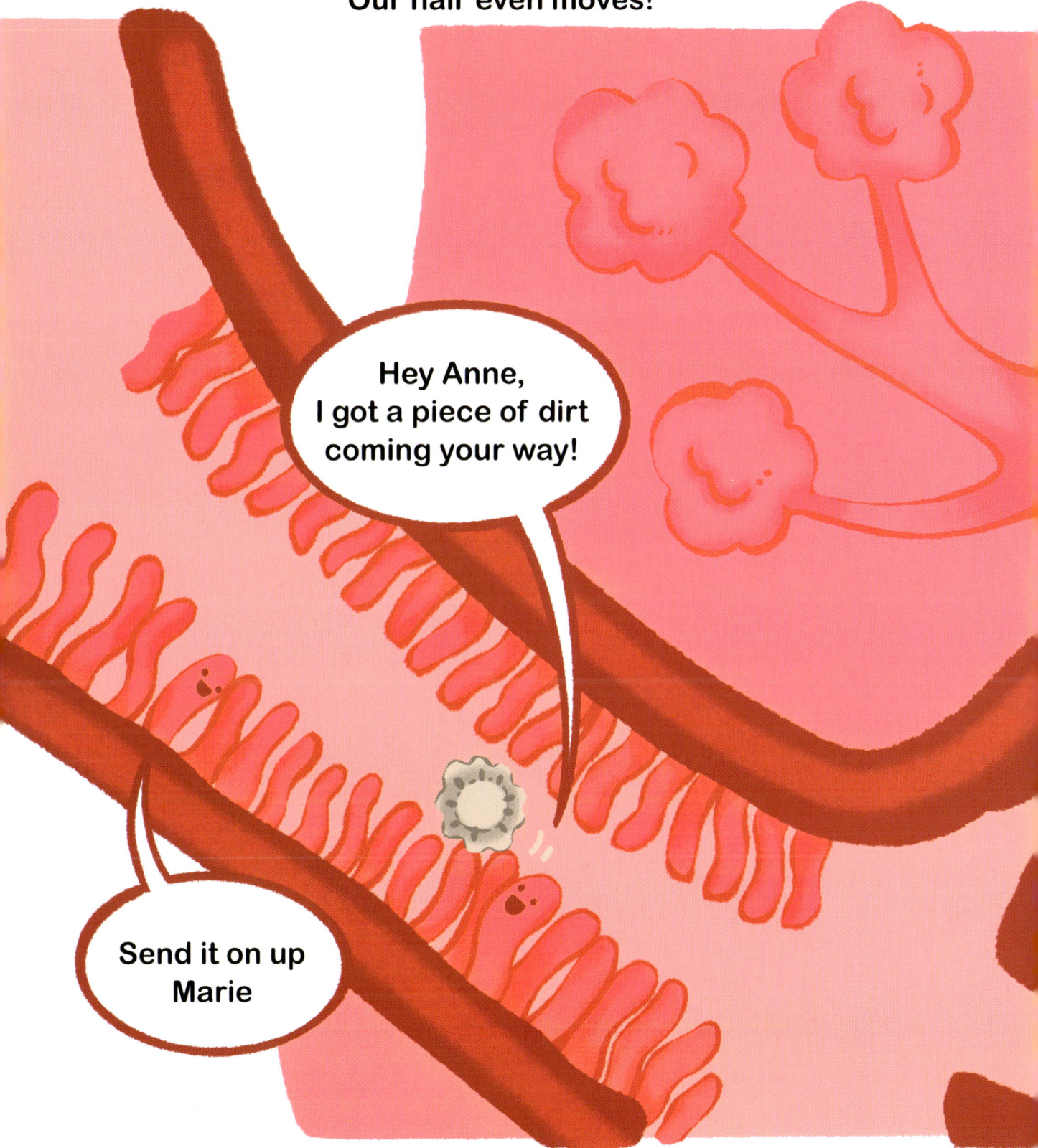

Hey Anne,
I got a piece of dirt
coming your way!

Send it on up
Marie

It's called cilia, and it tries to keep us clean of
dust and dirt by pushing it and the mucus out.

If we get sick from germs or too much dirt it can be hard for us to breathe.

That can make you sick and makes it harder for you to breathe too.

Doctors like to listen to your chest to hear your lungs.

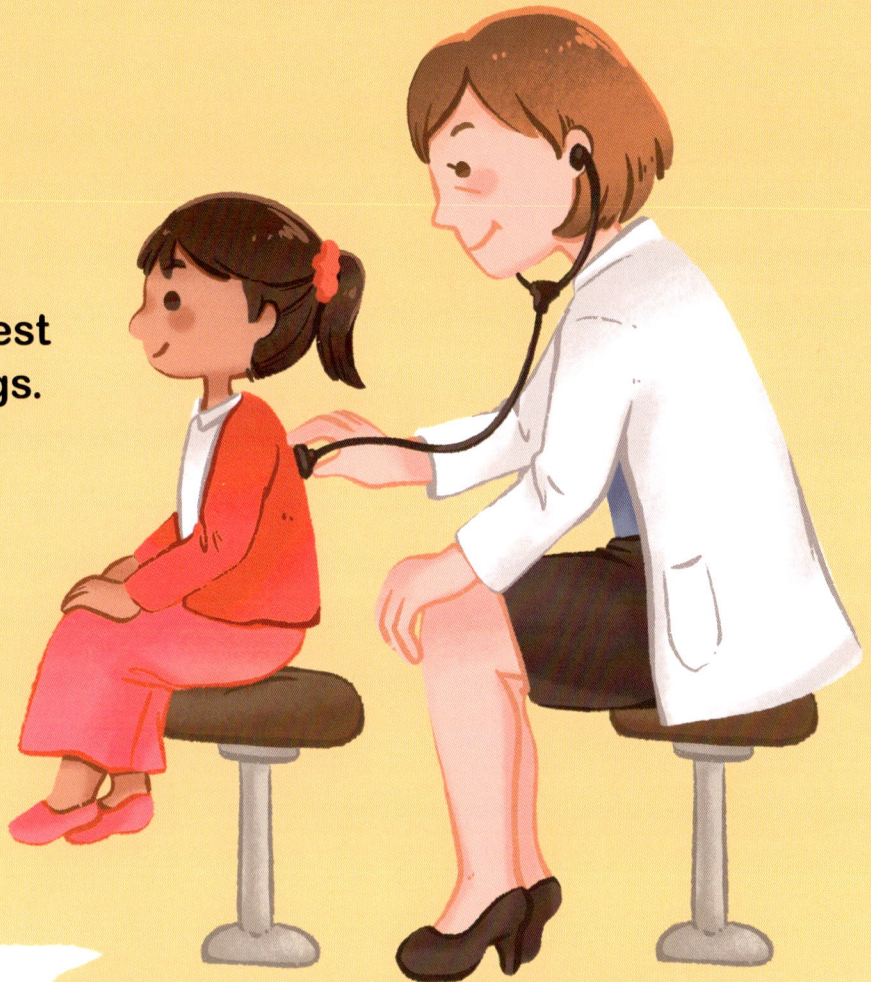

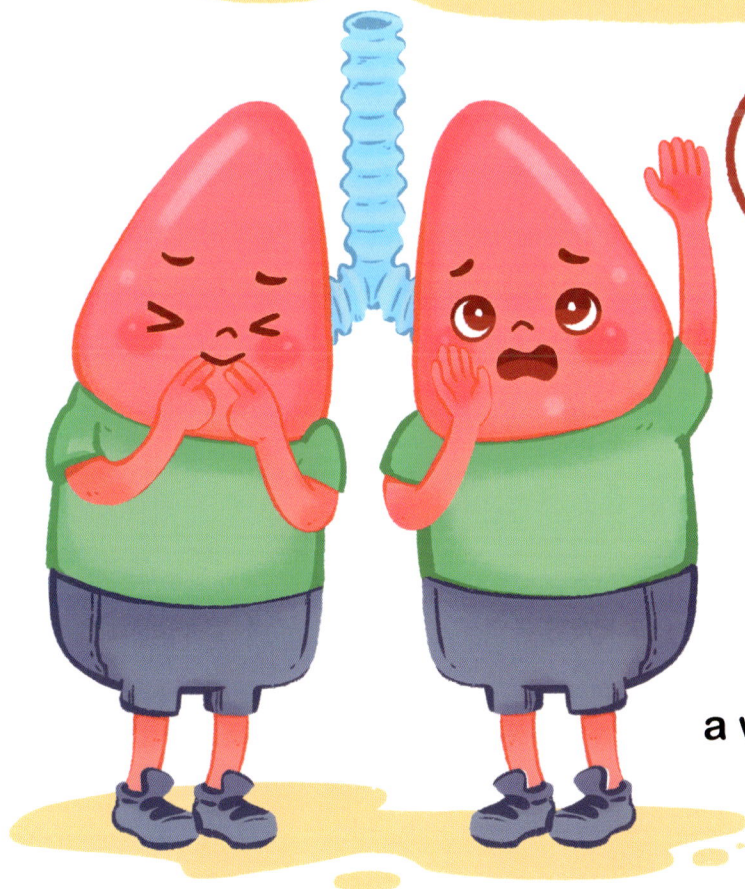

Help, we don't feel good!

Usually the lungs don't make much noise, but if you get sick they can sound like a whistle or little crackles.

We can even get hurt just like you.
If you get a bad enough bruise
on your chest or back it can
cause us to get bruised too.

That hurt.

It's already starting to bruise.

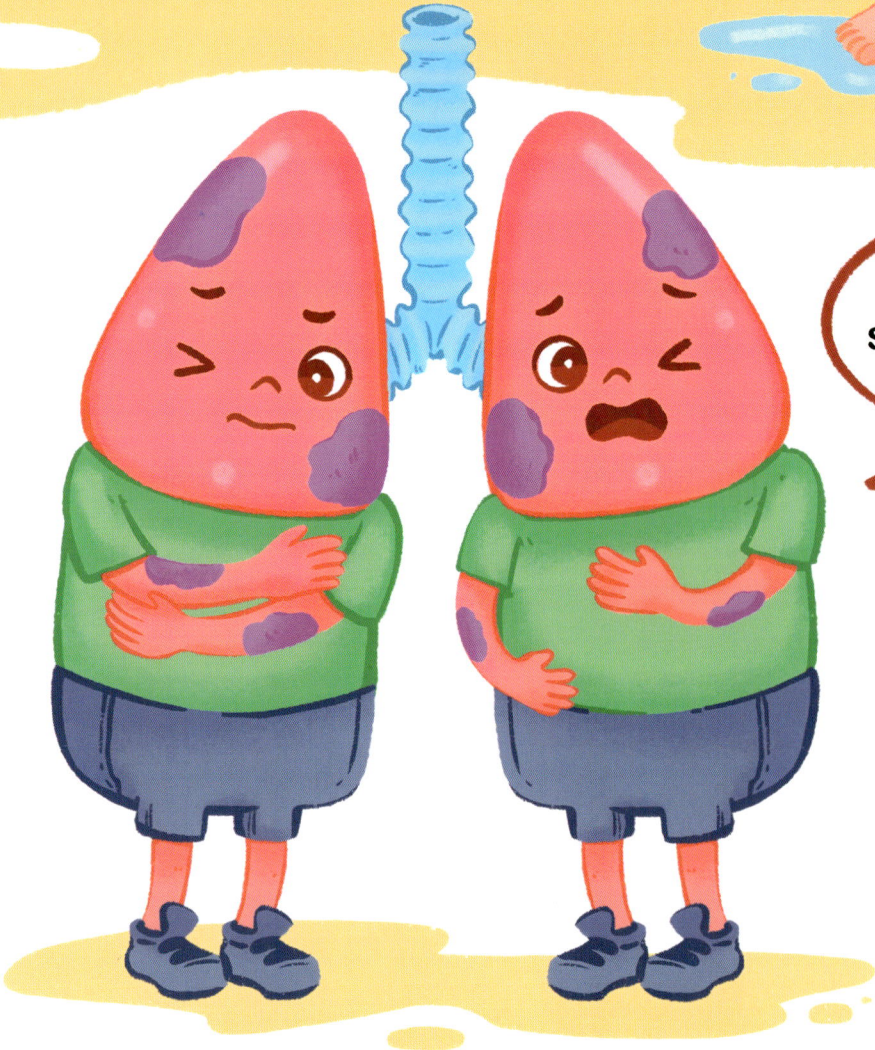

Sometimes one of us gets really sick
or hurt bad enough that we have to be taken out.
Don't worry though, even if that happens
you can still be a normal kid.

Even though you can do okay with just one of us,
it's better to keep us both healthy. Things like not smoking,
keeping our air clean, and wearing a mask around
sick people or keeping your distance
from them can help.

By working together,
we can stay healthy and keep having fun.

Alveoli –
Small sacs in the lungs
that let oxygen into the body
and carbon dioxide back out.

Bronchus –
The smaller tubes that
let air from your trachea
into your lungs.

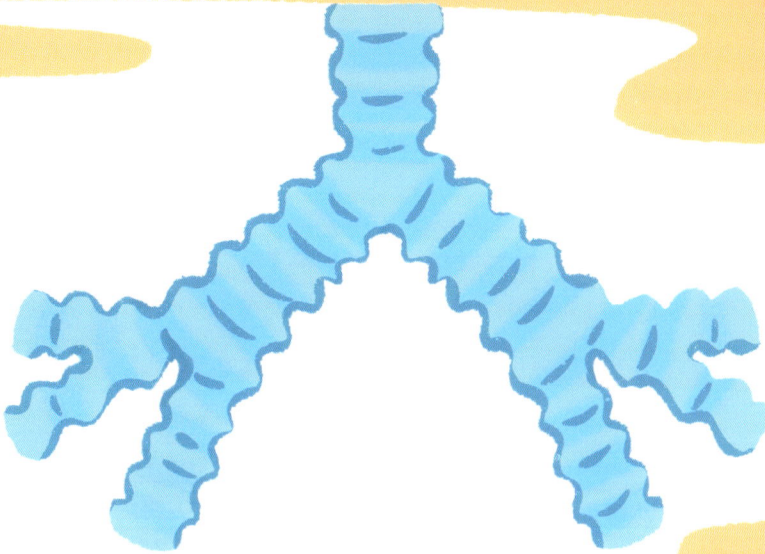

Carbon dioxide –
What your body releases
back into the air after using
the oxygen up.

CO_2

Cilia –
Hair-like structures that
stick into the lungs to help
move dirt and mucus out.

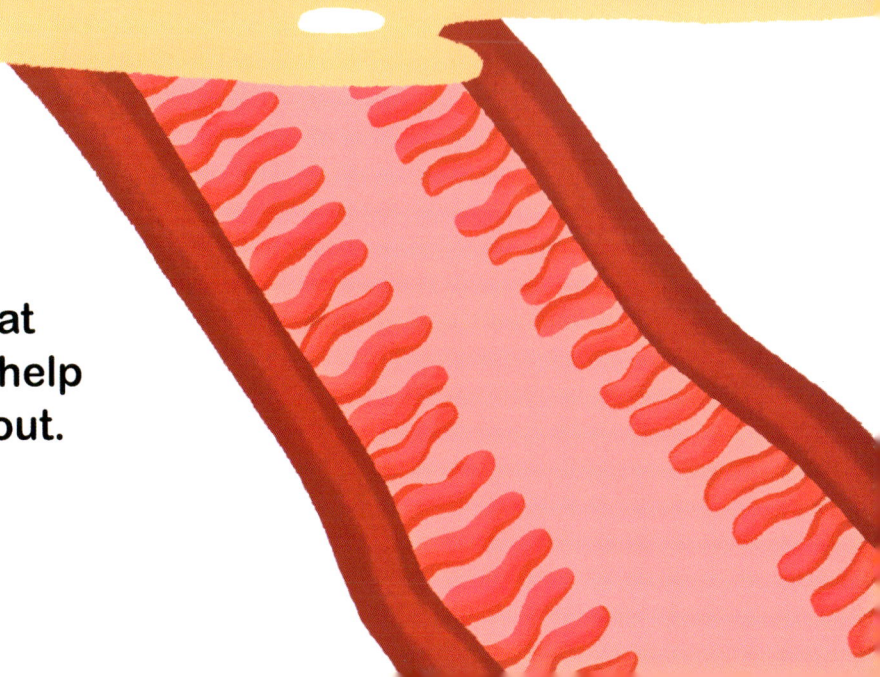

Mucus –
The boogery type of material that traps dirt and germs in your lungs.

Oxygen –
The part of the air that your body uses.

O₂

Trachea –
The big tube that lets air from your mouth or nose down towards your lungs.

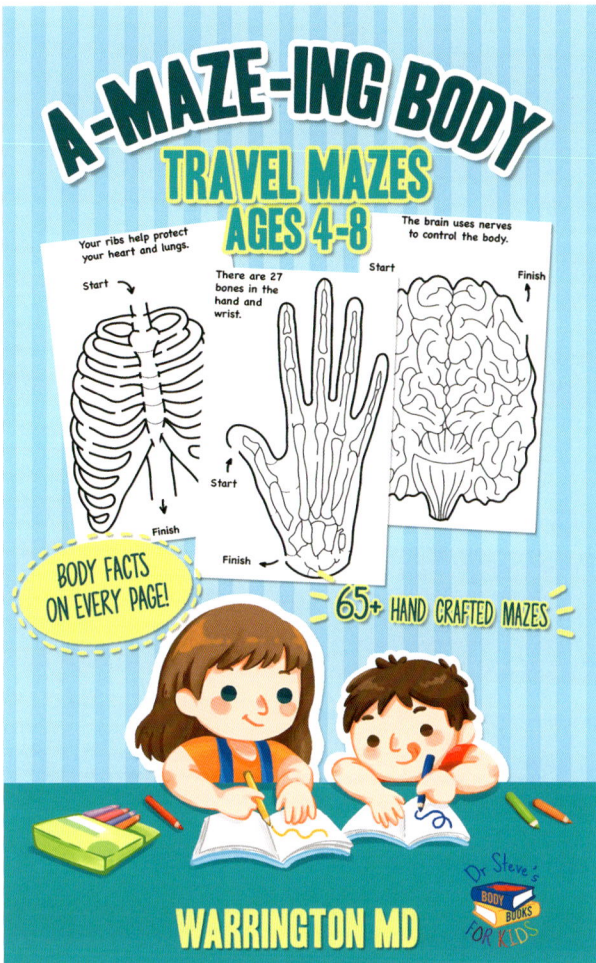

After you finish growing you will start to get shorter because of stress on your spine.

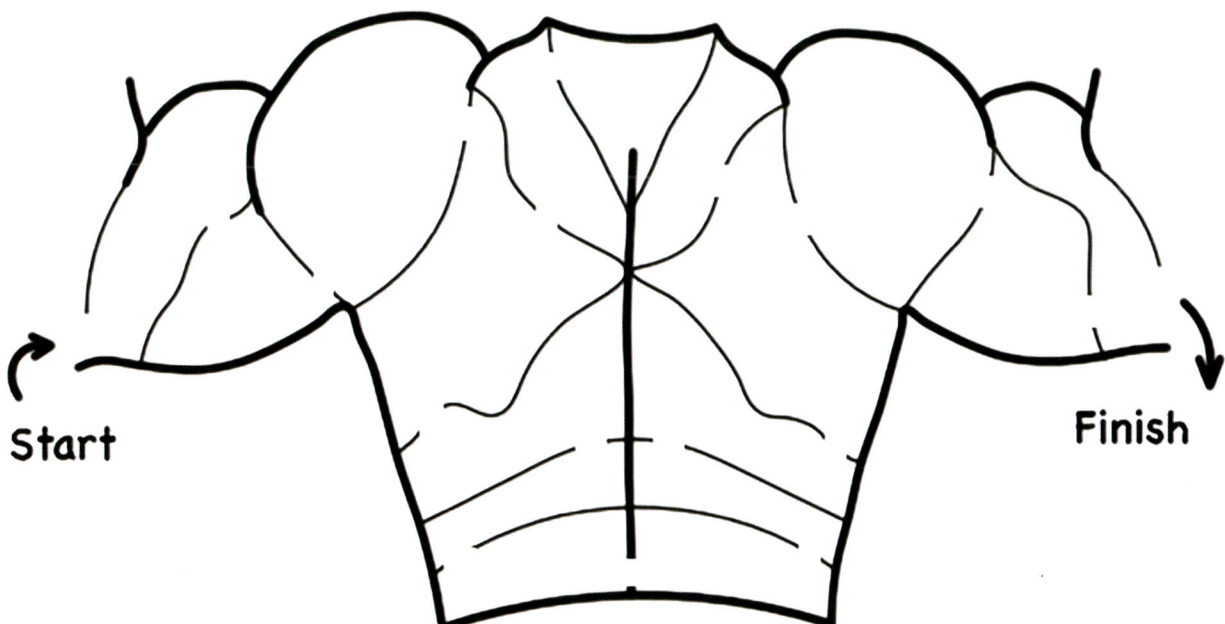

Start

Finish

Your intestines digest food.
They help absorb it.
That gives you energy to play.

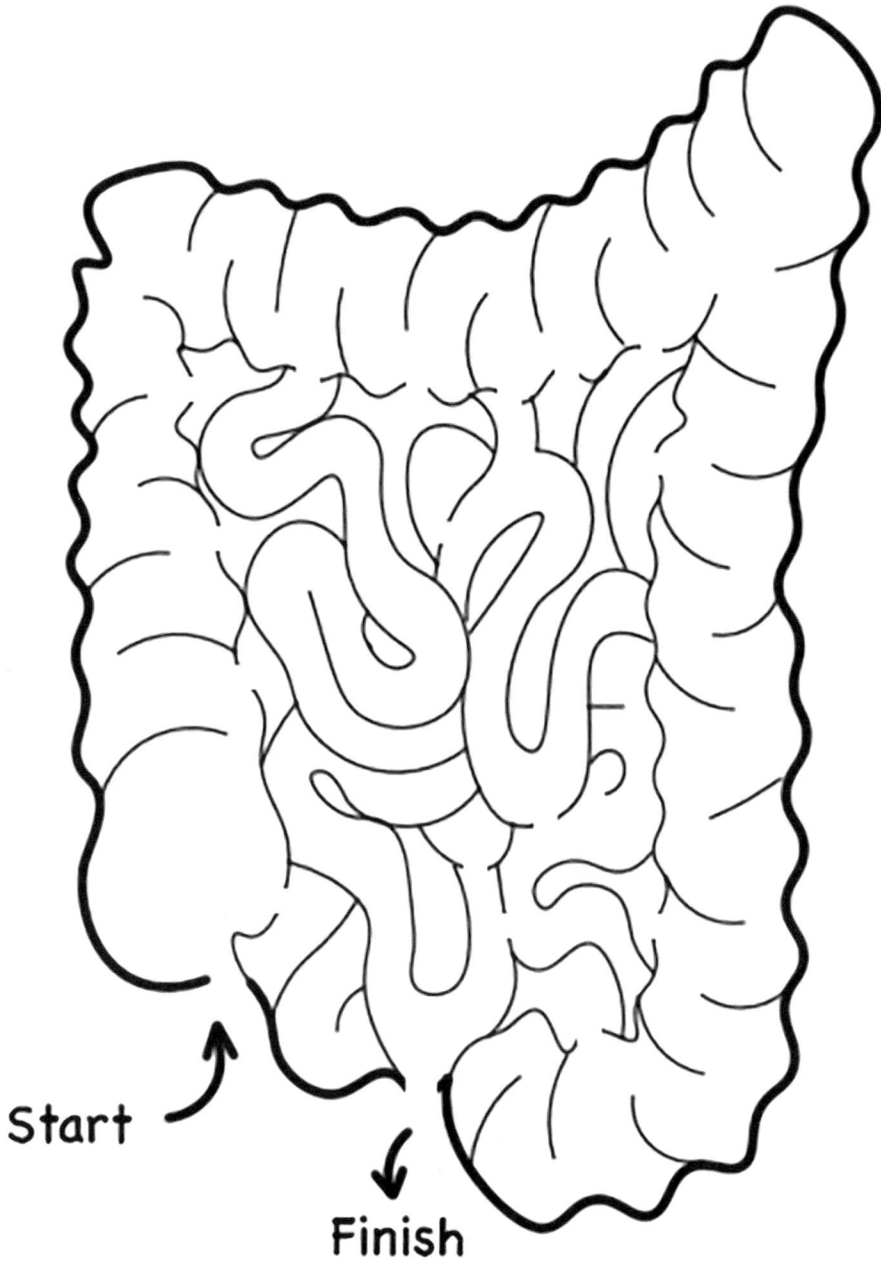

Start

Finish